G+Porter 6-12-93 £4.95

In the Steps
of
Chaucer's Pilgrims

In the Steps of Chaucer's Pilgrims

FROM SOUTHWARK TO CANTERBURY
FROM THE AIR AND ON FOOT

Jack Ravensdale

Aerial Photography
by
Aerfoto

SOUVENIR PRESS

First published 1989 by Souvenir Press Ltd,
43 Great Russell Street, London WC1B 3PA
and simultaneously in Canada

ISBN 0 285 62894 1

Photoset in Great Britain by
Rowland Phototypesetting Ltd,
Bury St Edmunds, Suffolk
Printed in Great Britain by
WBC Ltd, Bristol and Maesteg

To D.J.W

Acknowledgements

The author is indebted to the following for their help in providing information and advice about the places along the route taken by Chaucer's pilgrims: S. C. Humphrey, Southwark Local Studies Library; Ms Nicola Last, Local History Library, Greenwich; Miss P. M. Stevens, ALA, Local Studies Librarian, Dartford Central Library; Mr Colin Crook, BSc, ALA, Group Librarian, Central Library, Gravesend; Mrs Caroline Moorhead, BA Hons, ALA, Branch Librarian, Rochester Library; Mr Arthur Percival, MBE, BA, FSA, Honorary Director, Fleur de Lis Heritage Centre, Faversham; Mr David S. Cousins, Reference and Information Librarian, Central Library, Canterbury; Miss Wendy Newing, National Monuments Record; A. P. Sims, Air Photo Cover Photogrammetric Services, Ordnance Survey, Southampton.

In my own journeyings along the route, I was helped in photographing places of interest by Miss Jill Waterhouse and her brother Gowrie, whose enthusiasm and diligence in searching out more remote indications on the maps enabled us to discover many unexpected treasures. Mr John Crampton accompanied us on one occasion, stopping and starting to order with unfailing good humour, and several of his photographs appear in the book. Mr Marcus Blaber of Aerfoto showed a keen interest in the project, and his aerial photographs do much to pinpoint the ancient byways used by the pilgrims. I should also like to thank S. & O. Mathews, and the Museum of London for supplying photographs. The four maps on pp. 130–7 are based upon the Ordnance Survey 1:25000 Pathfinder maps with the permission of the Controller of Her Majesty's Stationery Office © Crown copyright.

Finally, my thanks to Leicester University Press for permission to quote from *Continuity and Colonisation* by Alan Everitt.

Contents

List of Illustrations

13

Fact and Fiction

Scholars who have tried to establish the route taken by
Chaucer's pilgrims are engaged in a process not unlike that of
Sherlock Holmes' fans who try to establish, by using the
methods of discovery attributed to the fictional detective, facts
of life for a man who had no real existence. The Baker Street
address given to Holmes by his creator was intended to give an
air of verisimilitude in the way that the Tabard was used by
Chaucer. In *The Canterbury Tales* the hostelry and the Host were
real enough. In Conan Doyle's writings Baker Street was a real
street, but the writer had to dissociate the address from too
much reality in the vain hope of preventing sight-seeing
readers from annoying real people living there. This he did by
giving the house a number which did not exist. The result was
that the respective authors were producing something that we
are more familiar with in the film world as 'feature
documentary', where fiction strays over the boundary of fact.

In literature this process offers the readers a new imaginary
rather than imaginative game, in which they continue the work
of the author by using people and places in the tales as new
names of local topographical features. Modern place-names in
Southwark draw heavily on Chaucer: the Tabard and Tabard
Street and Gardens; Becket Street, Pardoner Street, Manciple

15

Street, Prioress Street, etc. The Sherlock Holmes pub is a shrine, filled with manufactured relics of a rather more sophisticated character than those carried by Chaucer's Pardoner. The Tabard had changed its name to the Talbot and had been burned down long before modern scholars could fill it with literary relics.

Chaucer's characters in the Prologue to *The Canterbury Tales* are often so vivid that their author seems to have been drawing from life. There are touches of verisimilitude which have been fertile ground for Victorian scholars. They have identified and traced pieces of local colour which were obviously deliberately inserted by the poet to make the illusion more complete. Harry Bailey, Mine Host, for instance, seems genuinely to have been the name of the contemporary proprietor of the Tabard in Southwark. Some of the attempts to carry this further, suggesting that Chaucer was describing a single real pilgrimage in which he himself took part, are less happy. As the best manuscripts have come down to us, some major editing appears to be incomplete: Sittingbourne is mentioned before Rochester, although it is ten miles further from London. The transfer of some passages from one character to another sometimes leaves the sex of the speaker to be revised, and this has not always been done. The Second Nun, for instance, refers to herself as 'unworthy sone of Eve'.

Chaucer was obviously very familiar with the topography of the route, however, for he had lived and moved about in those parts. Whether or not he had been on a pilgrimage himself, he knew enough to convey a feeling of complete authenticity.

The Chaucer Society was founded in 1868, and its founder, Dr Furnivall, inaugurated an age of detailed examination of all the surviving evidence, in order to produce a text of *The Canterbury Tales* that was fully authentic and would bring us to the enjoyment of the actual words, and so to the mind of the man who wrote them. Henry Littlehales, his able follower, in 1898 drew together what was then established as the probable

The corner of Becket House, Southwark, showing how the area has been liberally bespattered, often incongruously, with names from *The Canterbury Tales*. Tabard Street runs down from Borough High Street where the Tabard Inn formerly stood. Becket House overlooks Tabard Gardens, along the bottom of which runs the most inappropriate appellation of all—Pardoner Street. *Photo: John Crampton*

17

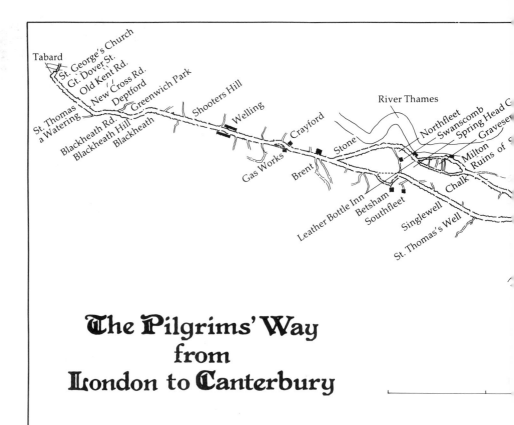

The Pilgrims' Way
from
London to Canterbury

The map made by Henry Littlehales to illustrate and clarify his book, *Some Notes on the Road from London to Canterbury in the Middle Ages*, published in 1898. The road he has uncovered is the line of the Roman Watling Street, and the places where the old road from London to Canterbury deviated from it. There were two stretches where he had to find a non-Roman

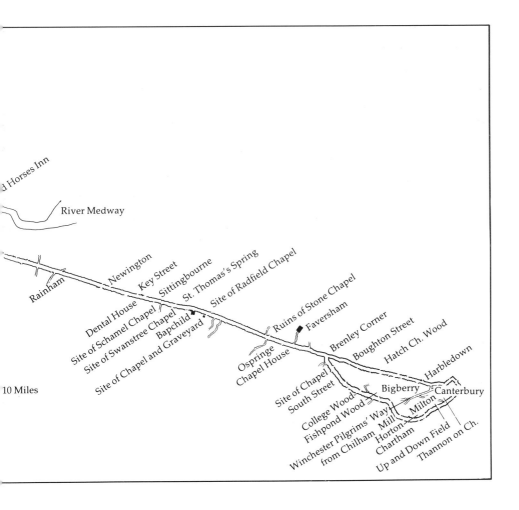

substitute—between Dartford Brent and Strood, and from Brenley Corner via Harbledown to Canterbury. In places, however, there were also alternative ancient, often prehistoric trackways which pilgrims might take when they seemed safer or easier than Watling Street.

19

route which Chaucer conceived his pilgrims as taking. The few scraps in the manuscript, and evidence such as was found in account rolls, added up to a road (see map) roughly on the line of the Roman Watling Street, with a few minor deviations. In the eighteenth century the name 'Pilgrims' Way' was attached to some of the other prehistoric tracks in southern England, forming a complex like a spider's web with Canterbury as its centre. This title, Pilgrims' Way, was not normally given to the route in Chaucer's mind, but seems to have been applied to the tracks followed by pilgrims from the Continent, coming and going to and from Becket's shrine mostly via Southampton or Dover. Thus the edible snails still to be found near the Dover Pilgrims' Way through Barham Downs are explained in Kentish lore as descendants of escapees from the supplies which French pilgrims took on their ways to the Shrine.

So Littlehales called his book *Some Notes on the Road from London to Canterbury in the Middle Ages*, and his first chapter 'The Route or Routes'. Yet even he slips into heading his map of the whole road from London to Canterbury, *The Pilgrims' Way*. It seems as if the word 'pilgrim' makes us automatically think first of Chaucer's characters. For us, the pilgrims' way *par excellence* is the route from Southwark to Canterbury, and in approaching the landscape through Chaucer studies we tend, unwittingly, to hi-jack in our minds the name of other prehistoric tracks for Watling Street and its subsidiaries. Be that as it may, the appellation was unknown in the Middle Ages, as indeed were most of the names of our Roman roads.

Littlehales was a scholar of some sophistication. He described his book about the road as an attempt 'to in some measure trace the route and tell something of the story of the road travelled by medieval pilgrims on their journey from London to the shrine of St Thomas Becket at Canterbury.' He began with several caveats:

First, where ancient roads run in parallel there is no way of determining which was most used by pilgrims.

Second, pilgrims may have taken a variety of different roads.

Third, safety may have caused pilgrims to divert from main roads to byways.

But where modern roads follow Roman roads without there being any trace of a former parallel road, he thought we might presume the existing road to be the pilgrims' way. This book sets out to explore that assumption and to discover, a hundred years later, what still remains visible of the medieval routes to Canterbury.

Pilgrims
Were They Alle

Whan that Aprille with his shoures sote
The droghte of Marche hath perced to the rote,
And bathed every veyne in swich licour,
Of which vertu engendered is the flour;
Whan Zephirus eek with his swete breeth
Inspired hath in every holt and heeth
The tendre croppes, and the yonge sonne
Hath in the Ram his halfe cours y-ronne,
And smale fowles maken melodye,
That slepen al the night with open yë,
(So priketh hem nature in hir corages):
Than longen folk to goon on pilgrimages
(And palmers for to seken straunge strondes)
To ferne halwes, couthe in sondry londes;
And specially, from every shires ende
Of Engelond to Caunterbury they wende,
The holy blisful martir for to seke,
That hem hath holpen, whan that they were seke.

The medieval pilgrimage began as a form of penance and, according to the teachings of the time, might help to shorten the period of suffering in Purgatory, through which all souls must pass. No one was free of original sin, and all must be so purged. But it seemed that penance and merit so acquired in this world might mitigate the punishment due to be paid after death. Sickness, too, in this world might be Divine punishment for sin, and prayers of the saints could intercede in Heaven on behalf of the sick sinner here below. From the start of his career as martyr, St Thomas of Canterbury was especially active in such healing.

In the Parson's sermon on the Seven Deadly Sins, which he gave in lieu of a Tale, he makes the point that for public sins the Church imposes public penance, hence the very public and severe penance imposed on Henry II after Becket's murder. The Parson might even have had Henry in mind: 'Commune penaunce is that preestes enjoinen men comunly in certeyn caas; as for to goon, peraventure, naked in pilgrimages, or barefoot.' Henry had dismounted at Harbledown, and gone barefoot to Canterbury in a pilgrim's shift. The Parson said further that satisfaction, a part of Penitence, stood most generally in alms and bodily pain. Henry had subjected himself to the most severe flogging by all the bishops and monks who received him at the Cathedral.

Opposite: The west end of St Nicholas Church, Harbledown, the point of departure for Henry II's penitential walk into the city of Canterbury. The old well at the rear of the church was later dedicated to the martyred archbishop. *Photo: Gowrie Waterhouse*

Overleaf: The ancient Stone Church, which lies only 100 yards from Watling Street just west of Ospringe. Although dating from Roman times, it was added to in the Middle Ages and would have been an important stopping place for pilgrims intending to spend the night at Ospringe.

25

Although the immediate effect of blood-shedding in the Cathedral was to desecrate it and make it unfit for divine service until it was reconsecrated, all these happenings in the long run heightened the spiritual powers of the place, and the route itself, with the passage of thousands of penitent pilgrims, acquired special virtue. Shrines, hospitals and chapels grew up more thickly here than anywhere else in the kingdom. Many of these in their turn acquired relics and powers to work healing miracles.

With a medieval saint it was possible to bargain in futures: sometimes a saint could be persuaded to intervene, heal or help in some other way in return for a promise to perform pious works, such as a pilgrimage to the saint's special shrine. In the Prologue to *The Canterbury Tales* Chaucer suggests that such bargains were the principal source of pilgrims on the Canterbury road. Many of the pilgrims of that time would have been able to understand the acquisition and loss of merit in a simple material fashion from the Doom pictures in their parish churches. As they looked east inside the church their attention would be riveted by the scene around the chancel arch. There, plain for all to see, were the souls on Judgement Day rising naked and sexless from the tomb, being weighed by the Archangel Michael, whose scales determined whom he would pass on to St Peter on the way to eternal bliss, and whom to the Devil, whose legions of demons were thrusting the damned, after binding them with red-hot chains, into the fiery, fishy jaws of Hell and endless torment. Such a fate was worth everything to escape from, and the exceptional powers of the martyred Archbishop offered special hope and promise. The tourist industry of the time boomed.

Hospitals were endowed as acts of pious devotion, their main purpose being, like a modern hospice, a refuge for the sick poor when terminally ill, but also, along the main routes, hotel accommodation for pilgrims who could pay, or better still, give charitable endowments. Some were even able to accommodate

The main surviving building of the *Maison Dieu* at Ospringe. Restoration work is still in progress, and this building is open to the public, under the aegis of English Heritage. *Photo: Jill Waterhouse*

royalty for overnight stops on their journeys. One such was the *Maison Dieu* at Ospringe, which contained a King's Hall in its complex of buildings. Tradition formerly asserted that it also contained a leper hospital, separated from the rest by a stream. Archaeological investigation in recent years has failed to confirm this. Romantic views of the past seem frequently to intrude the word 'leper' in front of any hospital, just as in parish churches any low side window tends to be called (wrongly) a 'leper window'.

Pilgrimage had its perils. A little removed from the bustle and din of Southwark's main highway were the isolated inns and other refuges for the underworld. How this network developed was described a century later by Thomas Harman, a magistrate in north-west Kent, in his book *A Caveat for Common Cursitors*. There was very high specialisation and division of labour amongst the rogues and vagabonds, whom Harman divided into twenty-four classes. Some in particular were active on the route to Canterbury, one staying overnight in Southwark and another operating in Dartford. The various types formed a hierarchy culminating in the Upright Men, who held power over the rest, and the Rufflers who aspired to promotion as Upright Men. They wandered between a network of tippling houses which only they frequented, scattered over half a dozen counties, with emergency hides in the woods where they could hole up in face of danger and be provisioned by their women-folk, morts (married) and doxies (unmarried).

The names of their trades were often descriptive as well as quaint: Demanders for Glimmer were mostly women who begged alms to help with their losses incurred by fire. Fresh-water Mariners, claiming losses from shipwreck, were similar. Harman says that most of their ships were drowned on Salisbury Plain. Abram Men were beggars who feigned madness. Counterfieit Cranks acted madness. Dummerers pretended to be dumb. All stole on the side. Hookers or Anglers carried long staves with wire hooks on the end, which they used to steal clothes and bedclothes through open windows.

They had a private language, too, some of which is still recognisable in Fagin's establishment in *Oliver Twist*. Kinchin Morts and Kinchin Coes, for instance, were little girl and little boy beggars under training in crime.

When the Canon's Yeoman is asked where he lives, his answer is revealing for one who has just joined the party:

> In the suburbes of a toun . . .
> Lurkinge in hernes and lanes blinde,
> Wher-as thise robbours and thise theves by kinde
> Holden hir pryvee fereful residence.

In other words: in the underworld.

At one point the probable route passed between Gadshill and Rochester. This was the spot chosen for an ambush in *Henry IV Pt 1* and Poins gives a good idea of the kind of hold-up on the highway that might be expected there:

> But, my lads, my lads, tomorrow morning, by four o'clock, early at Gadshill: There are pilgrims going to Canterbury with rich offerings, and traders riding to London with fat purses: I have visors for you all, you have horses for yourselves; Gadshill lies tonight in Rochester; I have be-spoke supper tomorrow night in Eastcheap; we may do it as secure as sleep: If you will go, I will stuff your purses full of crowns; if you will not, tarry at home, and be hanged.

The initial wait at the Tabard in Southwark was therefore probably to form a party big enough to feel the safety of numbers. Chaucer's pilgrims obtained a greater security: a fully armed knight with a squire. The Miller with more brawn than brain was a champion wrestler. The sly Reeve carried a sword, but its rusty blade could not add much to the travellers' confidence.

31

The other benefit derived from the rendezvous at the Tabard was to fix an entertainment programme. The importance of this for parties of pilgrims is revealed in Foxe's *Actes and Monuments*, purporting to be an account of an examination for heresy in 1407:

> . . . I know well that when divers men and women, that can well sing wanton songs, and some other pilgrims, will have with them bagge pipes: so that every town that they come thorow, what with the noyse of their singing and the sound of their pyping, and with them the jangling of their Canterbury bels, and with the barkyng out of dogges after them, they make more noyse then if the king came there away . . .

Such pilgrims were accused of 'wasting blamefully God's goodes, spendying thir goods upon vitious hostelars'. Thus were Harry Bailey's entrepreneurial skills discounted. The motives of the pilgrims were impugned: '. . . more to have here worldley and fleshly frendship then to have the frendshyp of God, and of his saintes in heaven . . ..

Chaucer's own attitude to pilgrims in general, including himself, was much kinder.

The Holy Blisful Martir

The story of Henry II and Thomas à Becket is one of the most dramatic of the whole of Christendom. The rise and fall of the hero, the turning of youthful friendship into defiant enmity, the horror of the murder provoked by the king who had himself been provoked beyond the endurance of medieval royalty, all heightened by the setting—the highest church in the land polluted by the murder of its own Archbishop within its doors—had all the appeal of popular melodrama, enhanced by the participants' high status.

Born in 1118, Becket, from humble beginnings as son of a city merchant, rose to become Chancellor, the highest office of state, by ability and the patronage of the Archbishop of Canterbury. As Chancellor he became the king's most loyal servant and personal friend. Henry wished to control his own kingdom more effectively just at the time when the development of Canon Law and the political ambitions of the Papacy were emphasising the rights of the Church *vis-à-vis* the secular rulers, and among rights claimed were undoubted abuses such as 'Benefit of Clergy'. This enabled criminals who had even the slightest degree of literacy to escape the death penalty by pleading that they were clerks and so exempt from punishment in the secular courts. The ability to read one verse from the Bible was accepted as proof. Equally obnoxious to the King was the

33

right churchmen claimed to appeal to the Papal court in Rome from the English courts.

To carry through his reforms, Henry, as a preliminary, decided to bring the highest posts of Church and state, Chancellor and Archbishop of Canterbury, into the hands of one man whom he could trust to follow the royal wishes. On the Continent the Emperor appeared to be finding such a scheme to work well in the Empire. Becket tried to escape this double burden, and warned Henry that if he became Archbishop he would no longer be able to be so complaisant to all the King's wishes. As he said later, as Archbishop he had authority over the King as well as a duty to him: 'You are my lord, you are my king, you are my spiritual son.' On becoming Archbishop in 1162, Becket resigned the Chancellorship.

Henry grew impatient, and tried to spell out the rights of the Church. Becket became defiant. The Pope was at war with the Emperor and distracted by the claims of a rival. Henry called Becket to face trial. Becket left England and went into an exile that was to last seven years.

Meanwhile Henry wished to make the hold on his dynasty more secure and wanted to have his son Henry crowned in his own lifetime. The custom was quite clear: only the Archbishop of Canterbury could officiate at a royal coronation. In the end Henry felt he had waited longer than enough and ordered the Archbishop of York and his colleagues to carry out the ceremony without Becket. The Pope was by now freer to help the exiled Archbishop, and a compromise was arrived at by a threat to place England under an interdict which would have shut all the churches with dire consequences for the country's life. In 1170, Becket returned home, on the way excommunicating all the bishops who had taken part in the coronation in his absence. The news reached Henry in Normandy. He interpreted it as undermining his dynasty and flew into a rage, suggesting that any loyal Englishman should get rid of Becket, if he wanted to serve his king.

The great cloisters in Christ Church Monastery have been rebuilt since Becket's time, but it was along these fatal walkways that he struggled back to his own church for the last time. *Photo: Gowrie Waterhouse*

The next act was pure Grecian tragedy. As the king and his courtiers sat drinking around the fire after dinner it was noticed that four knights were missing, and it was realised that they had taken the King's words literally and set out to find and destroy Becket. Those sent to intercept the four arrived at the coast too late to make the crossing to England: the tide had turned. Becket's pursuers caught up with him and, on 29th December, 1170, murdered him brutally on his way to Mass in his own Cathedral.

35

The whole of Christendom was appalled. The struggle of titans had come to this: the Primate of all England victim of a most sacrilegious murder. His old enemies could never stand their ground against this. As we have seen, the king, when he came back to England, had to walk barefoot from Harbledown into Canterbury and the Cathedral, and submit to flogging by a number of bishops and monks, as penance for his responsibility in the murder. Within hours of his death Becket began to work miracles, mainly of healing, but even political events were enhanced by the eye of faith. Becket was credited with the surrender of the King of the Scots on the day that Henry concluded his penance. His elevation to the rank of martyr was unusually swift. He became a champion of the rights of the Church: felonious clergy escaped the gallows for the rest of the Middle Ages.

The most serious weakness in his case for canonisation was recognised by some of his contemporaries, and was made the crux of T. S. Eliot's play, *Murder in the Cathedral*. He had been asked, 'My lord, would you be more than a martyr?' Orthodox Christian dogma made the fruits of martyrdom unobtainable by the will of the person involved. To seek or to court death as a martyr disqualified the seeker from that blessed state.

Gilbert Foliot, Bishop of London, who had opposed Becket's election to the Archbishopric and refused to make his profession of obedience to Thomas when he became Primate, had accused Becket of seeking to become a martyr by witchcraft, and he was probably the most able of Thomas's enemies. There was a strong element of jealousy in the opposition of London and York to Canterbury's claim of Primacy, and a strong sense of guilt at their failure to support Becket in his defence of the rights of the Church against the Crown, but the man they had regarded as a royal catspaw, helping the King to despoil the Church, had given his life defending the Church against the King.

By securing martyrdom—and this is indeed what Becket at

Pilgrim badges of St Thomas of Canterbury varied enormously, and tended
to be more elaborate than the simple scallop shell. The one shown here is
important because it has one of the very few remaining contemporary
representations of the shrine before it was destroyed on the instructions of
Henry VIII. The dead saint lies in full regalia with mitre and crozier. He can
be seen because the ropes and pulleys have raised the ark (the plated and
bejewelled lid). The little ships on the top may have some meaning in
relation to his long exile overseas. The flying buttresses may relate to
Canterbury Cathedral. *Photo: Museum of London*

37

times seemed to have intended, he acquired the ace of trumps against which all his antagonists were powerless. Even the King, who issued public disclaimers of any responsibility for the murder, had to perform that humiliating public penance.

It cannot surprise us that Canterbury quickly became one of the most important pilgrim centres in Europe. At first the King himself tried to claim half of any receipts at the shrine, but that was too much even for the twelfth century. The cathedral staff were even more eager. Immediately after the murder they mopped up all the saint's blood, diluting it with water. As they sold off little leaden ampoules of the blood, they maintained the level by further dilution, so that it could remain on the market until royal intervention stopped its sale at the Reformation four centuries later.

As part of this profiteering—one of the slightly incongruous results of the cult of Becket—there developed along the pilgrims' route, in places like Dartford, small foundries where lead was melted and cast into badges and trashy souvenirs, as well as the ampoules purporting to contain Becket's blood. Almost anything that could be sold to the tourist trade appeared in great quantities. Some palmers collected and displayed as many different badges as they could, rather in the way that some adults and children stick as many flags as possible all over the rear windows of the family car.

The scallop shell of the palmer was originally the badge of St James of Compostella in Galicia in Spain, but so successful were pilgrims who went there that it was adopted as THE general badge of pilgrims, especially of the professional palmers who

Opposite: The Altar of the Sword's Point as it appears today, in the room known as the Martyrdom. Although we have only a modern altar, and modern sculpture representing Brito's broken sword, a relief of the medieval altar can be seen in a panel above the west door, with the broken sword tip just visible. *Photo: Jill Waterhouse*

collected alms along the way, to finance the next leg of their journey. Lead survives well in the earth, and an astonishing number and variety of pilgrim badges, lost by their owners along the route, have lasted, to be found in later centuries. An excellent collection of them can be seen in the Museum of London.

At the centre of the new commerce was Becket's shrine. Crowds who came in the early hours and days after the murder forced their admittance, one by one, to the closed Cathedral. Three special places were devoted to the honour of the dead Archbishop:

First, the place of the martyrdom itself, in the north transept, including the Altar of the Sword's Point, where the sword of one of the four knights (Brito) had shattered on the pavement and been exploited by the Cathedral staff as a relic. The spot on the ground where the Saint's head is supposed to have fallen is marked by a slab, but since the paving stone here is alleged to have been improperly transferred to the nearby rival Benedictine house of St Augustine, it is better to remain sceptical. The present altar is modern, as is the sculpture above, in which the themes of Becket's murder by sword, and the Crucifixion, seem blended. The structure of the room, the Martyrdom, has been very much altered since Becket's day.

Second, where the body was left on the night of the murder, before the High Altar.

Third, the place of its first burial in the crypt.

As the international importance of the shrine grew, better accommodation for the saint became necessary. In 1220, Stephen Langton, Cardinal-Archbishop, arranged the Translation of the remains to another site. A new shrine was set up in the Chapel of the Blessed Trinity. Even today we can still see the

Opposite: The approach to Becket's Shrine in Trinity Chapel. The stone steps have been worn hollow by the feet and knees of pilgrims through the centuries. *Photo: Jill Waterhouse*

size of this shrine, destroyed four centuries ago, by the wear of the stone paving slabs and the stone stairs by pilgrims, on their knees for the most part, during the earlier centuries when the shrine was in use.

It was visited and described about 1500 by the Venetian, Polydore Vergil:

> The tomb of St Thomas the martyr, Archbishop of Canterbury, exceeds all belief. Notwithstanding its great size, it is wholly covered with plates of pure gold; yet the gold is scarcely seen because it is covered by various precious stones, as sapphires, balasses, diamonds, rubies, and emeralds; and wherever the eye turns something more beautiful than the rest is observed. Nor, in addition to these natural beauties, is the skill of art wanting, for in the midst of the gold are the most beautiful sculptured gems both small and large, as well such as are in relief, as agates, onyxes, cornelians, cameos; and some cameos are of such size that I am afraid to name it; but everything is far surpassed by a ruby, not larger than a thumbnail, which is fixed at the right of the altar. The church is somewhat dark, and particularly in the spot where the shrine is placed, and when we went to see it the sun was near setting, and the weather was cloudy; nevertheless I saw that ruby as if I had it in my hand. They say it was given by a king of France.

This great ruby was more probably a diamond, and was known as the Regall of France, having been given to the shrine

Opposite: The Corona, or Becket's Crown, the round chapel built for the Translation of his remains in 1220, to house the reliquary containing the portion of his scalp which had been cut off. It is at the very east end of the Cathedral and now contains St Augustine's chair, made of marble, on which the Archbishops of Canterbury sit for their enthronement. *Photo: Jill Waterhouse*

43

by Louis VII. It was later set in a ring which Henry VIII wore on his thumb. The base of the monument was of pink marble, about six feet high, with arched windows on all sides, through which the pilgrims could touch the coffin. The wooden ark containing the relics, plated and jewelled, rested on the marble. Over it was a gold wire mesh holding gold and jewelled ornamental offerings. Over all was a painted wooden cover which could be raised and lowered by ropes and pulleys. Around were seven great golden candlesticks. Erasmus tells how, on his visit to the cathedral, the Prior had the cover raised and identified the offerings inside, pointing to the items with a stick.

Below, in the crypt, the first tomb of the Saint remained, with the skull, and the hair shirt and drawers which had been found on his body, all lice-infested, proving his asceticism to his contemporaries. The part of the scalp which had been cut off was kept, after the Translation of 1220, in a reliquary of gold and silver in the Corona at the extreme east end of the church, known as the Crown of St Thomas. In some accounts the name of the chapel gets confused with the relic of Becket's scalp.

By Chaucer's time the effectiveness of pilgrimages and relics as money-spinners was beginning to dwindle. Parish churches for a time attracted a bigger share in pious endowments that might previously have gone to monasteries. There are signs that this trend was reversing again just before the Reformation. But Papal fund-raising by dubious means continued on an international scale. There was the traffic in Indulgences, for instance, by which, for cash down, the sinner might buy exemption from the penance due for his sins during a specific period. By 1520, in the reign of Henry VIII, when another Jubilee of Becket (the fifth) was due, it could not be celebrated because of lack of funds. If popular support was dwindling, Henry's rapacious eyes turned on the property of the Church which he had once championed, and not least upon the ostentatious wealth of the monks at Canterbury, where he himself had deigned to go on pilgrimage not long before.

Henry felt a great personal enmity towards Becket who had withstood the power of his King in defence of his Church. The strength of the monarch's hostility gave rise to the story, probably apocryphal, that Henry VIII instituted legal proceedings against Becket 368 years after his death, appointed counsel for both sides, and condemned him.

> Therefore his grace straytly chargeth and commandeth, that from hense forth the sayde Thomas Becket shall not be estemed, named, reputed, nor called a sayncte, but bysshop Becket, and that his ymages and pictures, through the hole realme, shall be putte downe and auoyed out of all churches, chapelles, and other places, and that from hense forthe, the dayes vsed to be festivall in his name, shall not be obserued, nor the seruice, office, antiphones, collettes, and prayers in his name redde, but rased and put out of all the bokes.

Wagons carried the loot back to the royal treasury in London. A Papal Bull later said that Henry had had the bones burned, and the ashes given to the winds to prevent any further veneration of his remains. The usually accepted account is that the bones were carelessly buried in an unmarked place nearby. In 1888 much excitement was caused when a coffin in the crypt was found to contain the bones of a tall man whose skull had been injured in a way that could have been the result of a blow like that which killed Becket. There is no proof. The mystery remains.

To Caunterbury They Wende

> Bifel that, in that seson on a day,
> In Southwerk at the Tabard as I lay
> Redy to wenden on my pilgrimage
> To Caunterbury with ful devout corage,
> At night was come into that hostelrye
> Wel nyne and twenty in a companye,
> Of sondry folk, by aventure y-falle
> In felawshipe, and pilgrims were they alle,
> That toward Caunterbury wolden ryde.

All travellers from the City of London and anywhere north of the Thames could only cross the river by London Bridge in Chaucer's time, and they would then turn right into Southwark, at that time a countrified suburb, to take the road for Canterbury, Dover and the Continent. Thus Southwark was strategically placed athwart the main trade routes and, with the cult of Becket, the pilgrim routes. Within this general commercial business it also became the metropolitan centre for the exchange of stolen goods, especially leather and metal.

It was especially appropriate that the pilgrimage described by Chaucer should have started at Southwark, as here was the Hospital of St Thomas founded by Becket's old rival, Gilbert Foliot, Bishop of London, after Becket's death. Becket had

1 The bridge over the Darent remains the centre of old Dartford, with Holy Trinity Church close by. The round-headed Saxon windows in the tower can just be seen above and behind the roof ridge. *Photo: John Crampton*

2 Above Swanscombe looking east. The disused railway line cuts across the top right-hand corner. Southfleet road, coming across from the left, goes under the now motorised Watling Street which forms part of the A2 (T). The central reservation alone is wider than the entire old Roman road would have been, but the general alignment is virtually the same, except for a reduction in the sharpness of the bend. The relatively sharp changes in sight lines of the Roman surveyor have been smoothed out into something longer for speed and much more gradual. The pylons with their long shadows and the overhead cables of the electricity Grid, converge from all quarters on to the large sub-station on the left. *Photo: Aerfoto*

Cobham from west to east. A series of five photographs illustrates the changes that a prehistoric trackway can undergo as it unfurls. *Photos: Aerfoto*

3 In the first picture, the approach to the village from the fields, the road is as straight as any Roman might have wished. Watling Street itself is some distance to the north, running roughly parallel when it has not been transmogrified too much into the A2.

4 In the next picture, there is a slight, but clear, change in direction. The road seems to shift its alignment to that of St Mary's, the parish church, very prominent near the upper right-hand margin. The college of chantry priests, founded in the fourteenth century, is at the lower end of the photograph.

1

2

3

4

5

6

7

8

9

5 In the third photograph, the most striking feature is the remains, after the hurricane of 1987, of the avenue from Cobham to the Hall. It starts from the lower margin, just left of the centre, and runs from virtually the end of the main built-up area of the village, diagonally up to where the Hall is almost hidden in the trees. The road that separated it from the avenue to run diagonally right, goes on as village street and woodland path.

6 The fourth photograph picks up the same greenway that had come out of the village street, going into the wood to the mausoleum in the top centre.

7 Finally, the way can be seen in the trees near the lower margin, leading towards the centre where all is blocked by the M2.

8 Inside Rochester Cathedral. The slenderness of the shafts and the delicacy of the rib vaulting produce in this Early English Gothic architecture a feeling of soaring to heaven which Norman work never attained. The pointed arch made true engineering in stone possible. *Photo: Gowrie Waterhouse*

9 View to the east to Rochester Bridge . . . The castle and Cathedral can just be made out on the far bank. The line of the greenway peters out at the main highway. *Photo: Aerfoto*

This engraving, more than a hundred years old, reveals rather more of the scale of Winchester Palace than we can see today, tucked away behind Southwark Cathedral and surrounded by high warehouses and modern buildings. This pattern of hall, through passages and serving end was common even in quite small dwellings, and survives today in many colleges at Oxford and Cambridge. Chaucer would certainly have known this building.

stopped in Southwark when he was making for London in 1170, on his return from seven years of exile in France. He had intended to spend the night at the Bishop of Winchester's Palace near St Mary Overy Dock. The Diocese of Winchester still reached the south bank of the Thames at this period, which was convenient for the Bishop as, like most of his colleagues on the Bishops' Bench, he found it useful to have a substantial town house in London when official duties called him there. Even today, despite the ravages of fire, bombing and other disasters, the ruins of Winchester House or Palace are still most impressive. What remains is the main hall, the heart of a large medieval house, with provision for large-scale entertainment, accommodation and administration. As part of his judicial work, the Bishop had a lock-up for offenders in his jurisdiction. It is from this prison in Clink Street, where the whole house stood, that the vulgar term 'to go to clink' derives its meaning. The ruins of the great hall, once hidden among wharfs, are now exposed again by the Blitz and redevelopment after the Second World War, and some restoration work has been carried out. The returning Archbishop never reached Winchester Palace. He was sent back by the Young Henry, who had been crowned by the rival bishops during Becket's absence. From then on the prospect of imminent death seemed to have accompanied him.

Close by the ruins of the Bishop of Winchester's Palace towers the Victorian Gothic pile of Southwark Cathedral. Although it has had cathedral status for only about 85 years, and the building as we see it is almost entirely Victorian, it is a firmly held tradition that there has always been a church on the site of St Mary Overy (St Mary across the waters) since the first coming of Christianity to these parts. The first records show a House of Sisters there, subordinate to Winchester. St Swithin, the ninth-century Bishop of Winchester, changed this to a college of priests instead, and in 1106 Canons following the Rule of St Augustine took over. Thereafter stability reigned, and the Canons continued to serve the church until the Reformation.

Early in the thirteenth century a major fire called for extensive rebuilding, and the style changed from the round arches of the Romanesque (Norman) to the pointed Gothic, known as Early English. Some fragments of this can be seen on the main porch,

51

Winchester Palace as it is today. We are looking into the main hall, and the three doorways facing us appear to be for serving from the kitchens across the screens passage. The floor of the hall has gone, and we can see into the undercroft, a semi-basement cellar used for storage. The fine rose window above has been restored relatively recently. *Photo: John Crampton*

The south side of Southwark Cathedral, showing the heavy Victorian contribution to its restoration. Despite a succession of disastrous structural failures and extensive repairs, pieces of the old stonework still survive.
Photo: John Crampton

53

A detail of the previous photograph, showing an example of the older work in the lowest courses near the South Door. The roughly dressed stonework in all probability belonged to the original church of the Augustinian Canons. *Photo: John Crampton*

and in some places fragments can be detected behind the newer work.

In 1469 the stone vaulting over the nave collapsed. Some of the oaken roof bosses from the new vaulting can be seen inside the church. Severe neglect of necessary repairs before the Reformation and, for a time, the letting of parts of it for secular uses (until the parishioners bought church and presbytery from James I), laid up trouble for the future. In the nineteenth century the remedies tended to be dramatic. The old Norman work, insofar as there was any left in 1835, was demolished, and in 1838 the medieval nave collapsed. In 1905 the expansion of London called for the establishment of a new diocese on the south bank of the Thames and the new Cathedral was born from the old riverside church.

There is much to be found in the interior, especially in the memorials. Chaucer's friend, the poet Gower, and Shakespeare's brother Edmund are buried here.

Chaucer is very parsimonious with references to places in the text, and this is as it should be. Such references are intended as a frame and not as a distraction from the Tales. The Tabard Inn, however, gets two mentions, and this establishes the Tales firmly in space and time. Can we assume from Chaucer's choice of this hostelry that it was the most popular among travellers gathering for a journey to Canterbury?

Southwark was rich in inns. Today, walking down Borough High Street from the present London Bridge, one passes a succession of inn yards clustered on the left-hand side between St Thomas Street and the corner turning off to Great Dover Street and the Old Kent Road—King's Head Yard, White Hart Yard, George Inn Yard, Talbot Yard, Mermaid Court, Chapel Court and Angel Place. Some survive in name only, but the George Inn remains as an impressive example of an old coaching inn. Chaucer describes the Tabard as being 'faste by the Belle', presumably another inn. The Tabard was the property of Hyde Abbey, near Westminster, in Chaucer's time. The building survived until 1676, when it was burned down and rebuilt as the Talbot. This remained until 1875. It must have been a substantial place, judging by the plan that has come down to us. There has been much redevelopment here in recent years, but in Chapel Court a timber-framed building has with-stood attacks from beetle, water, fire and the Blitz. Its five

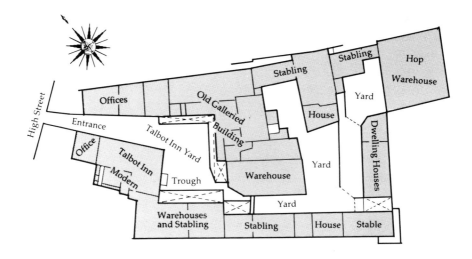

A plan of the Talbot Inn, a name which replaced the Tabard in the seventeenth century. It is said to have been completely destroyed by fire, but the plan of the yard with galleries around it follows what looks suspiciously like a medieval pattern. The ground-plan would not be as vulnerable to fire as would the timber-framed structures above. There would have been ladder-access to the galleries, and from them guest rooms could be reached.

mullions (the vertical timbers in a window frame) suggest a possible medieval origin.

*   *   *

Chaucer gave enough hints as to the topography of the pilgrimage to make us think that we can reconstruct the entire trip in imagination, with perhaps just one zone of much uncertainty between Dartford and Strood. Since he never completed the return journey and the Tales due on that part of the venture (or if he did the manuscript has been lost), those who would more fully understand the adventure that Chaucer dreamed up have to concentrate their efforts on the way from Southwark to Canterbury.

The route from Southwark out of London is still fairly easy to follow along the line of Watling Street. The first stop after Southwark was at the Watering of St Thomas. We are told that this was close to the second milestone on the Old Kent Road, at

A surprising survival in the heart of Chaucer's London. This timber-framed building in Chapel Court certainly suggests a medieval origin. The blocked-up window, with its five mullions, was quite a common pattern as the main window of a medieval hall. *Photo John Crampton*

Previous page: All that remains today of the 'Watering of St Thomas', at the corner of Albany Road and the Old Kent Road. The actual well where travellers would have stopped is said to have been where the Becket Arms now stands, and the water has now been used to create a welcome boating lake in this heavily built-up area. A small park surrounds it. *Photo: John Crampton*

the corner of Albany Road, and was so called from a brook or spring dedicated to the Saint. There is still plenty of water there, although no longer as vital as in the days of horse-drawn transport. There was a bridge built here in the Middle Ages, and this was in turn bricked up from its arches to form a culvert. It may well still be there under the road. What is very visible is the boating lake where the brightly coloured sails of the dinghies seem a far cry from the murder in the cathedral.

As the Chief Librarian of the London Borough of Greenwich has written, 'The route through London can easily be followed on any current street map.' This is testimony to how well the Roman surveyors did their work that those of us who have come after are content to follow. From Southwark we can go by the Old Kent Road, New Cross and Deptford Broadway; at Deptford Bridge we enter Greenwich. As the pilgrims pass through Deptford, the Host comments that it is 'half-wey pryme', that is, 7.30 a.m. Since they had risen at the Tabard 'whan that day bigan to springe', around 4.30 a.m., they have been nearly three hours on the road. Of Greenwich we have the Host's remark, 'ther many a shrewe is inne'. Since Chaucer's wife was living there at the time, and the views on marriage and wives in which the Tales abound are singularly unflattering, this is usually taken as a reference to her. Chaucer does not seem to have been happy in Greenwich where, in 1390, he was part of a commission to repair the dykes and drains. In his *Lenvoy de Chaucer a Scogan*, he contrasts the latter's good fortune in enjoying the King's favour at court, while he, Chaucer, is forgotten in solitary wilderness:

>Scogan, that knelest at the stremes hed
>Of grace, of alle honour and worthynesse,
>In th'ende of which strem I am dul as ded,
>Forgete in solytarie wildernesse.

Scogan is taken to be Henry Scogan, who became Lord of the Manor of Haviles after the death of his brother John in 1391, and who was tutor to the sons of Henry IV.

From Greenwich the main road climbs Blackheath Hill, crossing Blackheath itself at Shooters Hill Road, and the Borough boundary at the Royal Herbert Hospital, up Shooters Hill, and from there runs virtually direct to the approaches to Canterbury. The main road in Chaucer's time was more probably the one alongside Greenwich Park, rather than the present road across the Heath.

*　*　*

The country through which any traveller from London to Canterbury must pass was still very heavily forested in Chaucer's time. As well as the Great Weald to the south and west, and the Forest of Blean to the north and east, much of the downland had dense tree cover. Any roads through this might well run for miles alongside almost impenetrable woodland, or with such inhospitable country on both sides.

Early permanent settlement in Kent seems to have derived from the Dark Ages. Old large estates, 'original lands of the old kingdom of Kent', broke up into much smaller units, established on pockets of especially fertile ground in the valley bottoms. Beyond the borders of the land colonised in this way lay vast areas suitable for exploitation for the feeding of beasts. The marshes along the Thames estuary and near Romney in the south were great areas on which, in season, the flocks of farms and villages seated on higher slopes could be brought to feed.

Even more important were the dense oak forests of the Weald and the Blean, and also at that time of the downland. Here, the

In Chaucer's time much of the country around Watling Street would have been heavily wooded. This aerial view looking towards the Forest of Blean shows that thickly forested areas still remain in parts of Kent. The modern A2 runs across the bottom right-hand corner. *Photo Aerfoto*

harvest of acorns brought the village swineherds and their pigs, for the seasonal right of pannage. The beasts were fed from clearings, 'denns', as long as the acorns lasted. The placenames of Kent, Biddenden, Horsemonden, Shottenden, etc., almost map this phase of settlement. The woodland areas were also extremely useful for the seasonal feeding of the flocks and herds, not only on the grass growing around the tree-roots, but the foliage of the lower boughs as well. When these were cropped out of reach the herdsman could easily pull down more. In time these seasonal habitations became permanent as isolated farmsteads, 'Newingtons', connected with their mother settlements by twisting, narrow lanes, running up and down the steep hills and cutting deeply into the chalk on the downland. This pattern of colonisation, with small settlements widely dispersed and remote from each other, meant not only that the area would be thinly peopled, but also that the less desirable characters, the rogues and vagabonds, would be heavily over-represented.

The connecting lanes often linked not only the mother and daughter settlements, but also the ancient trackways that ran roughly along the contours, some of which have acquired the name 'Pilgrims' Way'. These hillside ways, which are thought to be of immense age, seem to have taken their origins in the Neolithic period, and to have been venerable before ever any Christian pilgrim appeared. The name *Pilgrims' Way* is clearly the result of the new function that they acquired after the murder of Becket when Canterbury drew immense numbers,. not only from 'every shires ende,' but also from the Continent, mostly via Southampton or Dover.

A strange feature appears from examining the whole length of the route from London to Canterbury and beyond on the early editions of the Ordnance Survey. Whereas long stretches of prehistoric trackway on the roads from Canterbury to Dover and Southampton are called *Pilgrims' Way*, the nearest that the road from Canterbury to London gets to such an appellation is a very short length on the final approach to the City, which is called *Pilgrims' Road*. This may well have been new road in Chaucer's time, constructed when the city Westgate was rebuilt as the main entry from London. Where the road emerges from Canterbury on the way to Dover, it is immediately designated *Pilgrims' Way*. The Survey seems to have assumed that Chaucer's pilgrims and others came straight down Watling Street, and its efforts on the London-Canterbury route are mostly to identify the road either as *Watling Street* or *Roman*

10 Rochester Cathedral: the interior of the west end. The simple but dignified lower stage Norman contrasts sharply with the highly decorated treatment of the external face of the doorway. In spite of this, the main window in the perpendicular style of the fifteenth century manages to fit in well. *Photo: Gowrie Waterhouse*

11 The keep of Rochester Castle towering above the curtain wall. Note the roundness of the nearest corner tower on the keep, the earlier square corner having been undermined and broken into by King John. *Photo: John Crampton*

Another sequence derived from a prehistoric track which survives as a greenway and in parts made-up road, leading from Newington towards Gillingham. *Photos: Aerfoto*

12 The first photo in this sequence is taken from Newington with its splendid three-gabled church, a fine example of a very typical Kentish type. Looking west, the road runs through the village from bottom centre, continuing onwards to the top left-hand corner.

13 The second picture, looking West-North-West from Gore Farm, picks up the greenway centre left, where it swings diagonally right past the power station, with Otterham Creek in the background.

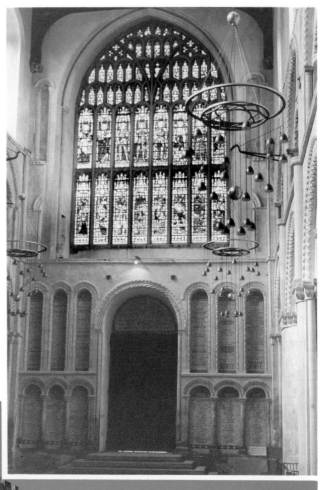

12

13

14

15

16

17

14 In the third picture the way can be easily identified running up from bottom left and swinging in towards the power station, before straightening again to run past Bloors Wharf.

15 Finally, we can pick up the way again as it runs past Bloors Wharf and continues in slightly sinuous curves, very typical of prehistoric tracts, into the distance.

16 From Tonge looking back towards Sittingbourne, Watling Street runs as straight as ever up the left-hand side of the picture, while the railway, on the old greenway, comes across from the other side, very close to serve the town with a station, and then swings out again. It would be difficult anywhere to find a clearer example of paired parallel tracks. *Photo: Aerfoto*

17 Faversham ahead and the railway again leaves the line of the old greenway, causing it to sink, for a time at least, to the status of a very minor road. On the right Watling Street pursues its straight line into the misty far distance. A clump of trees on the far side of a very chalky field on the right marks the site of the Roman mausoleum converted to a Christian church in the very early days of Christianity in England. *Photo: Aerfoto*

Road. The Pilgrims' Way proper, from Winchester, lies much further south along the scarp face of the North Downs.

The greater part of Watling Street can still be traced, even when parts of it are under the A2 and M2. North of Watling Street, and roughly parallel to it, the early editions of the Ordnance Survey show a considerable length of minor road, past Sittingbourne and Faversham. This seems to have been chosen for some stretches of the track when the railway was first built in the mid-nineteenth century, and the line still runs along it. Irregular pieces of woodland and rough ground at either side of the line give its origins away. The great expert on Roman roads, Margary, suggested that this and a similar way from Newington through to Gillingham, may have their origins as prehistoric track. This greenway may have ended its active life as a droveway which avoided payment of tolls on the turnpike roads. Another stretch of parallel road runs south of the Roman road, through Cobham, looping up to Rochester Bridge.

In his book *Continuity and Colonisation*, Professor Alan Everitt comments:

> As a rule the great Roman roads of England, like that which traverses the area between London and Kent, makes for a singularly unromantic countryside, and yet, for the student of history, they possess a certain kind of fascination, the beauty of a land long since begun.

Watling Street dominates the map of North Kent, but before the coming of the railway and the motorways its dominance was even more complete. The road engineers of the Roman Empire

Opposite: The modern approach to Canterbury from the west. This road may well be based on the new road created in Chaucer's time, when Archbishop Sudbury built the Westgate we still have today. The heights of Harbledown can be seen in the distance. *Photo: Jill Waterhouse*

laid out their alignments with impressive skill. Perfectly straight sections ran from siting point to siting point on adjacent hill-tops, producing the characteristically straight road that to the traveller looks straighter than it is. For the greater part of the route from London to Canterbury it is easy to spot the siting points on the Ordnance Survey map, or even from the slight bends in the otherwise straight road. The Roman surveyors, with very simple instruments, were able to do a most effective job, as long as the road user did not object to a climb to the top of every hill on the way. Margary, in his *Roman Roads in Britain*, lists the siting points from Harbledown to London, and fits them into the list that survives from imperial Rome, the *Antonine Itinerary*. Local conditions might mean departure from the ideal. Marshy ground, of which there is much between Watling Street and the Thames, and major river crossings caused diversions to suitable bridging points.

Watling Street points straight at the heart of London where, before London Bridge was built, the Thames was fordable at Westminster. Early in the Second World War its legend in Kentish folk lore was still growing. There was a firm belief that German air mail pilots before the war had learned how to follow Watling Street to London and Croydon Airport, and later returned to take their formations of bombers through to the capital. The Radar station at Dunkirk, on top of the hill at the end of Boughton village, was savagely dive-bombed on a sunny harvest afternoon at the start of the Battle of Britain. But the easiest approach for the Heinkels, Dorniers and Junkers was along the south side of the Thames Estuary. Old Father Thames

Opposite: As with so many towns, on this route, the lines of modern Dartford are inherited from Roman Watling Street. The Roman road runs straight downhill into the town centre towards the crossing of the River Darent. Recently traffic has been diverted, and the part of Watling Street leading through the heart of the town has been pedestrianised. *Photos: Jack Ravensdale*

was an infallible navigator, so long as the weather held! Perhaps we should include the Luftwaffe as pilgrims.

* * *

It is generally accepted that Dartford, fifteen miles from South-wark, would have been the first overnight stopping place for the pilgrims—a relatively easy first leg. There were in medieval times many inns along its main street where pilgrims could have found a welcome and a night's lodging. Modern Dartford, despite much rebuilding and a new ring road round the centre of the town, retains its basically medieval construction and a surprisingly large number of traces from Chaucer's time. Watling Street, now pedestrianised, cuts straight through the

Above and right: The heart of old Dartford, by the bridge. On one side of the river, a row of old buildings, on the other Holy Trinity Church. Saxon work can be seen in the tower with its small, round-headed windows.
Photos: Jack Ravensdale

70

town and the heart of the place remains the bridge over the Darent which still, after all the changes, has old buildings around it.

Bridges were a problem in medieval times, and a drain on resources for wayfarers. A favourite method of raising money to maintain a bridge was to attach a hermitage to it, where the hermit would collect money for the maintenance of his chapel and bridge. Both Deptford and Dartford, as their names suggest, began as fords, kept clear and maintained by hermits. The hermit at Dartford, licensed by the Bishop of Rochester, was installed by 1235, and would have ferried travellers across the river which was much wider than it is today. The footbridge does not seem to have replaced him until about 1410. Little chapels on or adjacent to bridges, now rare, would have been a familiar sight in Chaucer's time, thanks to the pilgrim traffic as a result of the Becket cult. Those on Watling Street would have to some extent competed for alms with Canterbury, but only to some extent; they might well have had the first chance to importune pilgrims who had come with sufficient alms in the hope of moving a very important saint.

A similar feature from the eighteenth and nineteenth centuries was the toll house on the turnpike roads. These were not unlike as methods of raising money for the transport system, but very different where the more modern were armed and contributions compulsory. As we move nearer our own time, public transport leaves more clutter, and our efforts to alter the landscape, to suit our more mundane requirements, do it monstrous violence. Those stretches of way parallel to Watling Street which had settled down as very minor ways until chosen for railway tracks were signs of things to come. In this century first the arterial roads and then the motorways slashed great gouges on the face of the countryside, and now, further south, all is devastation to feed the Channel Tunnel. It will help with the modern idea of pilgrimage to beaches and unwashed Mediterranean sand.

The rear of the house which is said to have been the home of Wat Tyler, one of the leaders of the Peasants' Revolt of 1381. *Photo: Jack Ravensdale*

73

The former Dominican nunnery in the grounds of the Ironworks at Dartford. Little remains to be seen of the medieval stonework, and what we have is an elegant Tudor dwelling house in red brick—far better than the destroyer of the nunnery deserved. *Photo: Jack Ravensdale*

A relic from the Dominican nunnery—a portion of the medieval wall that once surrounded the nuns' precinct. Monastic houses had extensive grounds which preserved open space inside the growing town. *Photo: Jack Ravensdale*

Holy Trinity Church, which is built very near Dartford bridge, dates from Saxon times and, despite much alteration over the centuries, shows Saxon work in the partially Norman tower with its small, round-headed windows. On the opposite side of the bridge, running back from the road, are some of the oldest houses in the area, including one which claims to have been the home of Wat Tyler, one of the ringleaders in the Peasants' Revolt of 1381. He certainly was a Dartford man.

In the Ironworks stand the remains of the Dominican Nunnery, probably the only house of this order in the country. At the Dissolution of the Monasteries it was rebuilt in a very handsome red brick as occasional lodgings for Henry VIII on his travels to and from the Continent. Part of the old wall round the nuns' precinct is still standing, running out to the arch that carries the railway line.

75

Perhaps the best example of Chaucer's search for realism comes in the introduction to the *Man of Law's Tale*, on the morning of the second day of the pilgrimage. Our Host gives date and time, by using the shadows of straight trees to measure the declination of the sun.

> Our Hoste saugh wel that the brighte sonne
> Th'ark of his artificial day had ronne
> The fourthe part, and half an houre, and more;
> And though he were not depe expert in lore,
> He wiste it was the eightetethe day
> Of April, that is messager to May;
> And sey wel that the shadwe of every tree
> Was as in lengthe the same quantitee
> That was the body erect that caused it.
>   And therfor by the shadwe he took his wit
> That Phebus, which that shoon so clere and brighte,
> Degrees was fyve and fourty clombe on highte;
> And for that day, as in that latitude,
> It was ten of the clokke, he gan conclude.

This is given us as the Host using very simple science in a field where Chaucer, author of the *Treatise on the Astrolabe*, was an expert. Such fragments as Chaucer gives to enable us to work out the general progress of the pilgrims are just sufficient to suggest a possible timetable to Canterbury on the outward journey, without making it certain.

Probably the interpretation in most favour currently suggests that the cavalcade, following its overnight stop at Dartford, would have pressed on to Ospringe (31 miles further on). Neither of these is mentioned in the text, but the *Maison Dieu* at Ospringe had been developed for the very purpose of providing accommodation for a party of pilgrims who could pay their way. Its rating, with a *Camera Regis* or King's Hall, qualifies it to take the highest in the land.

This leaves a day's double journey, calling for a stop between the two. Rochester would fit in nicely from the point of view of simple mileage, but scholars have usually taken the Host's injunction to the Monk:

> Lo! Rouchestre stant heer faste by!
> Ryd forth, myn owene lord, brek nat our game,

to mean that the story-telling went on as the pilgrims rode past Rochester. Furnivall, however, gave a third overnight stop at Rochester and, for good measure, a break for dinner at Sittingbourne.

There are, of course, since Chaucer has been so sparing with placenames, other parishes where Watling Street, the main road, passes through. For instance Cobham, between Dartford and Rochester, whose church had been newly restored in Chaucer's time by Sir John de Cobham. Sir John had also built a college or chantry for five priests that they might say masses for the souls of his ancestors. The buildings were converted to almshouses after the Dissolution of the Monasteries and remain so today. The church contains a unique series of memorial brasses of the Cobham family, dating from 1320 to 1529. This might not have attracted Chaucer as much as it attracts us.

Beyond Dartford, aerial photography above Swanscombe clearly shows a change in the alignment of the main road, where the present A2 diverges from Watling Street. The relatively sharp changes in sight lines of the Roman surveyor have been smoothed out into a wider and longer curve, to allow for greater speed. The line of the old road is still visible, however, running across the fields to converge with the new main road as its curve flattens out.

The main diversion during the Middle Ages in this part of

Overleaf: The medieval almshouses at Cobham. Built by Sir John de Cobham in 1362 as a college or chantry for five priests, they have been in use as almshouses since the Dissolution. *Photo: S. & O. Mathews*

18 Faversham from Watling Street, looking north. The Creek, winding in from the River Swale, can be seen top right. This access to the sea was the key to the town's growth and prosperity. The Creek is navigable to modest craft, and the medieval warehouses on the quay speak of a thriving trade from an early date. As in so many towns dominated by a powerful monastic foundation, the Abbey may have controlled this commerce. The town grew up entirely on the east bank of the Creek, but has now expanded to engulf the parishes of Davington and Preston. Davington Priory stands out, set on a rise slightly to the left and above Faversham Creek. *Photo: Aerfoto.*

19 A row of immaculately restored houses in Abbey Street, Faversham. *Photo: John Crampton*

20 Boughton High Street (Watling Street, now relieved of traffic by a bypass), showing the rich, warm colours of the local materials that have been used for building. *Photo: Jill Waterhouse*

21 Boughton Interchange from the air, clearly showing how the main trunk road has been curved away from Watling Street to divert the flow of traffic from Boughton. There is a change of alignment in Watling Street at this point, but it straightens out again as it runs towards the bottom of the picture. *Photo: Aerfoto*

18

19

20

21

22

23

24

25

22 The end of the bypass that began at Boughton, looking west. Watling Street, now a quiet country road, runs straight as a die to Dunkirk and on to Boughton, while the new curve in the A2 meets up with the Roman road again at either end. Just off Watling Street, in a stubble field on the right, stands a pylon where five stood before the Battle of Britain. *Photo: Aerfoto*

23 Looking towards Willows Wood and Church Wood, west of Harbledown, the A2 again diverges from Watling Street, which runs on above it. From the ridge in the top left-hand corner, a track leads down to meet Watling Street. This interchange is the beginning of the tangle of new roads that passes through Harbledown to Canterbury. *Photo: Aerfoto*

24 Looking towards Harbledown and beyond to the suburbs of Canterbury (Chaucer's thropes end) which would have been far less extensive than they are today. St Nicholas' Church and the almshouses where Erasmus came as a sceptical pilgrim can be seen top centre. *Photo: Aerfoto*

25 St Nicholas' Harbledown seen from the valley bottom. The end of the row of almshouses appears to the right of the church. *Photo: Gowrie Waterhouse*

Watling Street was where the road to Swanscombe, Northfleet and Gravesend forked. The medieval road from Dartford Brent to Strood effectively took over the status of main road from this section of Watling Street, which was degraded into a mere by-way or even footpath until the coming of the arterial road earlier this century. After passing through Gravesend, which had acquired great importance by the thirteenth century at the latest, as the end of the Long Ferry from London, the left-hand road, going towards Canterbury, eventually rejoined Watling Street at Strood on the approach to Rochester with its bridge and High Street part of the main Roman way. The name itself, *Strood*, is another variant of the commonest Roman word which more frequently appears as a placename in the guise of strate, streat or street. In Damascus Paul lodged in a street which was called 'strait'.

There were other problems later from chalk quarrying which, undermining the cliffs, made the road unsafe between Northfleet and Gravesend. Before the end of the seventeenth century there is a description of a new road 'set back from the waterside to the east of Gravesend town'.

Even if we can establish the line of Watling Street, the loop roads and parallel ways would have allowed the pilgrims choice according to weather and road conditions, or simply as they felt inclined. Flooding from the northern marshes would have produced temporary local diversions. We cannot now be certain precisely what route Chaucer's pilgrims took in his mind, but something like an established pilgrims' way may have been

Opposite: Rochester Bridge, seen from the top storey of the Castle keep. The view over the river with the bridge at the first crossing point upstream makes it easy to sense the strategic importance of this site, which the Romans discovered and exploited. When first built the window surrounds of the keep would have been neatly finished off with round heads and possibly some decorated mouldings. *Photo: Jill Waterhouse*

recognised soon after Becket's cult became effective. For the first fifty years after the murder, Becket's Feast was celebrated on the anniversary of his death, 29th December, in deep winter, when the Roman roads may have been very difficult as they traversed the valley bottoms. In 1220, on Becket's Translation, 7th July became his main feast, and his pilgrims and their leaders, like Harry Bailey, may have come to recognise the advantages of the new season or even its precursor, the spring, for an open route along the hillside. By Chaucer's time the main motive for a pilgrimage could have been enjoyment.

At Cobham, south of Watling Street, a very clear minor road runs parallel to the main highway and may well have been used by pilgrims wishing to pause for refreshment or to avoid the ill-maintained antique Roman road on its approach to Rochester bridge. In modern times roadworks on that part of Watling Street revealed the old Roman road and showed that a causeway had been built which had foundations of four-foot-long oak piles with baulks of oaks laid transversely over them. Over this were layers of flint, ragstone, chalk and gravel to carry the roadway clear through the river mud, which was eight and a half feet thick at that point. In spite of the elaborate construction method and grouting of the top layers with mortar, the surface appeared to have been very rutted, and, in a bad season, on the more open sections of the road at least, pilgrims may well have found the hillside tracks on the chalk downland more attractive.

Today, the road through Cobham approaches and runs through it as a made-up village street, shifting its alignment

Opposite: Rochester Cathedral seen from the Castle. In spite of later modifications, the overall feeling is emphatically Norman. When this was built, most large monastic churches being constructed at that time in Europe would have shown a marked family likeness to Rochester. Few have retained much of this through the changes of the intervening centuries. *Photo: Jill Waterhouse*

slightly to approach the parish church of St Mary and running out of the built-up area towards Cobham Hall. It then fades into a woodland path, winding off to the M2, where suburban development obliterates it on the approach to Rochester bridge.

*   *   *

The best way to approach Rochester is by train. As the traveller comes in towards the bridge, the two dominating features of the city, the Castle and Cathedral, appear to be moving in a slow dance, as they emerge and disappear in turn behind the shops and houses and move slowly to and fro, seemingly around each other. The bridge at Rochester had a key strategic importance in former times, providing as it did a route across the Medway that avoided the marshes.

Rochester Cathedral had a predecessor, or rather a series of predecessors, from AD 604—that is to say, there was a cathedral there for far longer before Chaucer's time than since. A substantial amount of Rochester Cathedral fabric that is standing today would have already been centuries old when Chaucer came by, and much more of this Norman work would still have been standing safely in his lifetime. Probably what preserved so much of this English Romanesque (that is, Norman) when other parts were rebuilt in the modern style of the thirteenth century (Early English) was the rivalry with Canterbury. As the see of the Archbishop, the Primate of all England, Canterbury was much more attractive to pious bequests than a cathedral of a Suffragan see, Rochester. Rochester's best effort to outdo Canterbury by finding a saint of its own was very far from producing another Becket. William of Perth, a Scottish baker who had come on pilgrimage, was overtaken and murdered by

Opposite: The west door of the Cathedral, again very typical of its period. The series of orders (the term used when a doorway recedes in a series of concentric steps) is capped by a low relief carving of Christ in Majesty. *Photo: Jill Waterhouse*

robbers on his way home. His body was brought back and buried in Rochester Cathedral. Then the miracles began. This was about the year 1201, midway between Becket's murder and his Translation, that is, between the two strongest fund-raising ventures launched in the name of the Saint. Like Canterbury and so many other English cathedrals, Rochester was served by a house of Benedictine (Black) monks, and although a good deal of the space previously occupied by the monastery was built over again after the Dissolution, those spaces that were saved leave room from which the church can be seen and admired.

The building patently contemporary with the nave of the cathedral is the square Norman keep of the castle. When first built this was in the forefront of military fashion, and the interior decorations show that it was intended for an important residence as well as static defence. But the weakness of this design soon became apparent at Rochester as elsewhere. Square corners were vulnerable to undermining by sappers and battering rams. In 1215 King John's forces broke in at the south-eastern corner. The internal defences in depth were so good that the besiegers were ejected again. The replacement for the tower that had been undermined is round, and has no vulnerable corners.

The City of Rochester is rich in Roman and medieval history, as well as its association with Dickens in more recent times. An Edwardian local historian, Edwin Harris, suggested that pilgrims in Chaucer's time would have stayed at the Crown Inn which dates from the early fourteenth century, but there is no direct evidence for this.

Opposite: The north aisle arcade of the Cathedral. This is high-quality Norman work where variations in the treatment prevent the massive effect from being too overwhelming. Not only can the passage in the thickness of the wall (the triforium) be seen, but also the greater window space in the top storey (the clerestory), whose function was to light the nave. The height is a further way of reducing the heaviness of this Romanesque (Norman) style. *Photo: Jill Waterhouse*

The Norman keep of Rochester Castle towers above its massive curtain wall, with the gateway on the left-hand side as an added defence. Together they make a formidable structure that commands all approaches. *Photo: Jack Ravensdale*

Once past Rochester, an unnamed stopping place for refreshment occurs in *The Canterbury Tales*, when the Pardoner is called upon to tell his tale:

> 'But first,' quod he, 'heer at this ale-stake
> I wol both drinke, and eten of a cake . . .
>   . . . but I mot thinke
> Upon som honest thing, whyl that I drinke.'

Rochester Castle: the tower gateway into the bailey (the defended enclosure surrounded by the curtain wall in which the keep stands). We can see here some signs of modernisation early in its life: the lower courses covering the foundations are splayed out to make any heavy stones dropped by the defenders bounce off at unpredictable angles towards any besiegers who ventured too close. *Photo: Jack Ravensdale*

91

As can be seen from this interior view, the keep at Rochester Castle shows a sophistication in its architectural decoration, and probably originally in comfort, that was extremely rare in Norman castles. The quality is better than that in Dover Castle. The keep is divided horizontally into separate halls, and the elaborate fireplace and finish of the stonework suggest a building that was meant to be lived in as well as defended. *Photo: Jill Waterhouse*

Looking through an archway in the bailey wall of the Castle to the west window of the Cathedral. This was one of the ways in which the Normans brought Church and state together, by physically putting the Cathedral in the shade of the Castle. *Photo: Jill Waterhouse*

93

This sounds like a country ale-house, suitable for refreshment while thinking out a story. Could it have been Rainham or Newington? It was between Rochester and Sittingbourne, and the latter must have been some way off, judging by the angry taunt of the Summoner to the Friar shortly afterwards:

> Quod this Somnour, 'and I bishrewe me,
> But-if I telle tales two or three
> Of freres er I come to Sidingborne.'

It is impossible to know what was in Chaucer's mind. His timetable seems still unfinished, as does his more general arrangement and revision, and incidents like the Pardoner's demand for a drink and a snack could not help the schedule to keep a tight rein.

It is, however, at this point that the former greenway from Gillingham comes close to Watling Street, passing through the village of Newington, and this might well have been a route chosen by the pilgrims in preference to the Roman road. Seen from the air, looking west from Newington, the course of the greenway can still be picked out, running past the splendid three-gabled village church, through fields and on as a minor road through a succession of villages above Otterham Creek and Bloors Wharf as it curves in towards the Medway.

Moving on towards Sittingbourne, the parallel road to the north, now appropriated by the railway line, stands out clearly as a former greenway, swinging in towards Watling Street at Sittingbourne itself and then curving away again on the other side of the town. Milton Regis, west of Sittingbourne, was once a royal manor, and its Court Hall still exists, now moved to the high street. Restoration work has made use of old timbers from elsewhere where necessary. Quite close to the railway beyond Sittingbourne, at Deerton Street, with only one farmhouse nearby, stand the ruins of a little church, with most of the massive walls of the first stage of the tower still in place. The unevenness of the ground to the left of the tower, the site of the

The fifteenth-century Court Hall at Milton Regis, moved to a more open site and rebuilt, using old timbers where repairs were necessary. In the Middle Ages courts and their procedure were used not only for the administration of justice and the punishment of crime, but also for such activities as audit, estate management and general administration. *Photo: Jack Ravensdale*

former nave, suggests that much is still here for the archaeologists. In Chaucer's time this could have been a stopping place of importance for pilgrims.

*   *   *

As Watling Street progresses towards Ospringe, the greenway again emerges, abandoned by the railway line to curve off towards Faversham as a very minor road and bridle path. Much closer to the Roman road and just west of Ospringe lie the ruins of a unique church, known today as the Stone Church, whose central cell has been identified as a former Roman mausoleum dating from pre-Christian times. The Roman walls, incorporating tiles and dressed stone, are clearly visible. The church was consecrated to Our Lady of Elwarton in the eighth century, and

26 Harbledown: the Victorian almshouses, which replaced the medieval leper hospital, nestle on the hillside below the church and graveyard. *Photo: Jill Waterhouse*

27 Approaching Canterbury on the main road, the Cathedral rises shimmering white in the distance. This view would have greeted Chaucer, but less spectacularly without the Bell Harry Tower. *Photo: John Crampton*

28 Christ Church Great Gate, splendid as it was on the eve of the Reformation. *Photo: Gowrie Waterhouse*

26

27

30

31

29 The sunny south side of Canterbury Cathedral from inside the Great Gate. *Photo: John Crampton*

30 The ruins of the Infirmary, a feature of all Benedictine monasteries, not only for the sick, but also for the regular bleeding inflicted on the monks for their health. *Photo: Jill Waterhouse*

31 Canterbury Cathedral from the air. The Cathedral appears to float in a sea of green shade. The boundary of the precincts shows up dramatically, and the Great Gate, low down in the centre, marks the place where the life of the cloisters came in touch with the outside world. Most things we can see would have been different in Becket's time, although some would have been familiar to Chaucer. *Photo: Aerfoto*

The church at Milton Regis reflects the village's former proud status as a royal manor. There is a rich range of styles and features of interest, and some lively restoration work, such as the tracery in the decorated style in the large west window to the right. *Photo: Jill Waterhouse*

The ruined tower of the church that stands alone in a field north of the railway at Deerton Street. An excavation of the ground to the left would surely lay bare the ground plan of the nave. *Photo: Gowrie Waterhouse*

its east end, with sanctuary and altar, is still recognisable. It has been a ruin since about 1530. All along this part of Watling Street are hints of continuity between late imperial Rome and the Dark Age successor Kingdom of Cantium. It was to the Christian Queen Bertha of Cantium that Augustine came in 597.

A view of the east end and central cell of the Stone Church near Ospringe. The sanctuary and altar are still easily apparent, as is the Roman construction of tile and brickwork in the cell to the left, showing as clear stripes in the wall. Thanks to the presence of Queen Bertha of Cantium, and her group of Christians at court, the transition to Christianity may have been smoother as well as earlier here. *Photo: Jill Waterhouse*

Scholars are agreed that Chaucer intended his pilgrims to spend their last night on the journey at Ospringe, and they would undoubtedly have stayed at the *Maison Dieu*, a remarkable medieval survival on the A2. Two buildings remain of what was once a much larger complex, straddling Watling Street and forming a medieval hospital and hostelry. It had its own royal suite, the *Camera Regis*, and was in fact used by royalty going to and fro on the road to Canterbury and Dover or London. It was formerly thought to have had a leper hospital in a building detached from the main concourse by a stream running

The splendid *Maison Dieu* at Ospringe, showing the two remaining buildings separated by a lane. The royal suite, or *Camera Regis*, was in a part of the complex now lost, on the other side of Watling Street which runs past in the foreground. The main room on the ground floor of the restored building contains much evidence of Tudor improvements, in its handsome stone chimney piece and pargeted ceiling, at present being restored to its former glory. *Photo: Jill Waterhouse*

through the site, but archaeological excavation failed to find anything at all that could have confirmed this.

The two surviving buildings each have a stone undercroft which contains thirteenth-century work, but some of the stonework has been reset. Above, in the building to which the public has access, is a splendid crown-post with moulded capital and base, sitting on a moulded tie-beam. The official

The crown-post roof in the room on the upper floor. This has been strengthened by metal rods running through the beam on which it rests.
Photo: Jill Waterhouse

Details of built-in cupboards of venerable date in the walls of the upper floor. *Photo: Jill Waterhouse*

guide book dates this as from the reign of Henry VIII, although it probably could have been earlier. It also suggests that these two buildings had their origins as houses for two chantry priests. Certainly two such priests were appointed in the latter days of the hospital. A considerable amount of Roman pottery has been found by archaeologists, and this is now on display to the public.

Immediately to the north of Ospringe lies Faversham, whose wide market street, wharves and creek give it away as a

Glass cases displaying the wealth of excellent Roman pottery on display in the upper room. *Photo: Jill Waterhouse*

medieval inland port of some standing. It was a 'Limb of the Cinque Ports' in the Liberty of Dover, which meant a very privileged town with substantial powers of self-government. All along Watling Street villages tended to grow up but not to expand. This happened with Ospringe, in spite of its importance in the tourist trade. Faversham, however, was able instead to develop its commerce to something far greater because of the nearness of the River Swale with its facilities for trade. The town as we see it today does not take us all the way back to Chaucer's time, although he would have recognised the layout of the central, older part and the wide Abbey Street running from the Abbey (now completely ruined) to the church and fed commercially from the docks by Quay Street. The Abbey was founded by King Stephen in 1147, to serve as a royal mausoleum. He was buried there in 1154. Arden's House stands here, where, it is said, Thomas Arden, one of the local profiteers from the Dissolution of the Abbey, met his death. He was murdered at

A row of beautifully restored houses in Abbey Street, Faversham, part of an award-winning scheme. *Photo: John Crampton*

Arden's House, Faversham, where Thomas Arden, the sixteenth-century profiteer, was murdered at the behest of his young wife and her paramour, Mosbie, in 1551. The crime was recorded by Holinshed and formed the source for the play by an unknown writer, *The Tragedy of Mr Arden of Feversham*, which was published in 1591. Some scholars have attributed it to Shakespeare, who is known to have visited the town; others favour Marlowe, whose father was a native of nearby Ospringe. *Photo: John Crampton*

the instigation of his much younger wife in 1551 and became the subject of a drama published in 1591.

Davington Priory, on the west of Faversham, was a Norman foundation destroyed at the Dissolution. The church survived and is still in use, and part of the domestic quarters remain, now the home of Bob Geldof, KBE, and his wife Paula Yates.

* * *

The following morning Chaucer's pilgrims set out from Ospringe and we are now on surer ground, for he becomes

106

The church of St Mary Magdalen at Davington Priory, formerly the nave of
the Priory Church, with its Norman doorway. On the right are the
surviving domestic quarters, now the home of Bob Geldof, KBE. *Photo: Jill
Waterhouse*

107

more generous not only with placenames but with indications of time.

> Er we had riden fully fyve mile,
> At Boghton under Blee us gan atake
> a man, that clothed was in clothes blake . . .
> His yeman eek was ful of curteisye,
> And seyde, 'sires, now in the morwe-tyde
> Out of your hostelrye I saugh you ryde.

Boughton, where the pilgrims encountered the Canon and his Yeoman. Old Watling Street runs straight through a village lined with magnificent timber-framed houses. Those shown here come from all periods and vary in style, but live in the harmony of architectural good manners. *Photo: Jill Waterhouse*

In this house the black timber studs occupy as much of the frontal area as does the white plaster, except where some change in style at the right side suggests rebuilding in the past. *Photo: Jill Waterhouse*

Here, at Boughton under Blean, the party receive their final reinforcement, the Canon's Yeoman. The Blee or Blean from which he emerges was the great forest of north and north-east Kent. Watling Street runs right through the village, but the A2 has been diverted and now runs round it, rejoining Watling Street just past Dunkirk. There is no certain answer to the problem of preserving or rescuing our village landscape from intolerable pressures of heavy traffic. It is not always clear when a cure is a cure.

In this area, between the Weald and the Blean, there has been no shortage of timber to restrict local builders. The High Street of Boughton, lined with timber-framed houses of all periods, makes use of oak timber both structurally and decoratively, so that in some houses there is as much timber showing as plaster. Local clay has been used to give the rich, strong reds of the bricks and tiles, and the village seems literally to have grown out of the ground, and to speak to us in a strong Kentish vernacular.

* * *

> Wite ye nat wher ther stant a litel toun,
> Which that y-cleped is Bob-up-and-doun,
> Under the Blee, in Caunterbury way?

Of all the indications of real places that Chaucer gives in the *Tales*, that which has given most rise to argument must be Bob-up-and-doun. Modern scholars seem satisfied with Harbledown. The village is so hilly that any journey in or through it involves much going up and down, and it fits in very well with the distances travelled in the various stages of the journey. Attempts to identify it with an 'Up-and-down' field on the far side of the river are unconvincing. Erasmus, when on his sceptical pilgrimage to Canterbury in the early sixteenth century, with his friend John Colet, certainly approached the London Road by way of Harbledown Hospital:

> Then as we went toward London, not far from Canterbury we came in to a great hollow, and a strait way moreover

Opposite: a detail of one of the houses in Boughton High Street, revealing something vital to our understanding of vernacular buildings: they develop and change over the years. On the right a door seems to have been moved and its old space blocked up. A door that size would have taken a lot of draughts with it. *Photo: Jill Waterhouse*

110

The hospital at Harbledown where, in the early sixteenth century, Erasmus was accosted by a beggar who threw holy water, proffered a shoe upper to be kissed as a relic of Becket, and held out a bag on a pole for cash. The bag on the pole seems to endorse the belief that this hospital at least was one for lepers, unlike so many that have been falsely so described. It may, however, have been intended to make it easier for a horseman to give alms. *Photo: Jill Waterhouse*

112

bowing so down, with hills on either side, that a man cannot escape, nor it cannot be avoided, but he must needs ride that way. Upon the left hand of the way there is an almshouse for old people; from them runneth one out as soon as they hear a horseman coming, he casteth holy water on him, and anon he offereth the over leather of a shoe, bound about with an iron hoop, wherein is a glass like a precious stone. They that kiss it give a piece of money.

This piece of shoe was supposed to be a relic of Becket. Colet was outraged, but Erasmus, feeling sorry for the old man, gave him a small piece of money.

Rolling mid-Kent seen from Harbledown hospital, with the Victorian almshouses on the right, descendants of medieval forebears. This undulating countryside could well have given Harbledown its name Bob-up-and-Down. *Photo: Jill Waterhouse*

An old road into Harbledown, from hospital to farm. *Photo: Jill Waterhouse*

Even today almshouses, rebuilt in Victorian times, nestle
below St Nicholas church, where Erasmus saw their predecessors. It was the sole survivor of three hospitals which
Lanfranc, the Archbishop of Canterbury, founded for lepers in
about 1084. Some of the stone in the church there would have
been carved about that time, to judge by its style of decoration.
Although many medieval hospitals are falsely ascribed to use

114

for lepers, the one at Harbledown may well have been so in its early days, sited well out of town, and thus reducing the risk of infection.

The old well at the rear of the church was dedicated to St Thomas and was otherwise known as the Black Prince's Well. Both the church and hospital were dedicated to St Nicholas.

The features of Harbledown that gave it its nickname in Chaucer's time were still visible there in the eighteenth century, as described by Hasted, the great antiquarian and topographer

Modern motorways are creating 'lost' tracks faster than either medieval or prehistoric pilgrims ever did. Here, near Harbledown, a few hundred yards from the A2, disinherited lengths of old road and byway seem to have lost all purpose in a few years. *Photo: Jack Ravensdale*

of Kent. After noting that it was known for the pleasantness and salubrity of its air he continued: 'The whole is very un-equal ground of frequent hill and dale, affording continued picturesque and pleasing prospects over the neighbouring country.'

It is still very exciting to come out of the narrow by-roads of

The Westgate, new in Chaucer's time, built by Archbishop Sudbury to replace one of great age, which had fallen into ruin. It was at this time that the new approach road to the city was built, the Pilgrims' Road. *Photo: John Crampton*

Harbledown on a sunny afternoon, on to the main road, and see the west front of the Cathedral, shimmering white in the distance. Here we have some advantage over the pilgrims of the fourteenth century: Bell Harry Tower was not there in Chaucer's time, but then neither were the concrete street lamps. The City's Westgate had been rebuilt by Archbishop Sudbury in Chaucer's time, and with this the normal route of the pilgrims into the City had changed. Today it has changed again. New, fast highways carry traffic towards the city, and around the hospital and church at Harbledown short lengths of older, narrow ways linger on without much of their former function. But they are the link between us and the past. This is where Henry II set off on his barefoot penitential walk to the Cathedral, and down this track Erasmus undoubtedly came in his guise as a sceptical pilgrim. And in a nearby field are echoes of a still older past: crop-marks that suggest the work of prehistoric man.

* * *

As the pilgrims make their way down towards Canterbury, Chaucer gives us another demonstration of his expertise in measuring the angle of the sun to gauge the time of day.

> By that the maunciple hadde his tale al ended,
> The sonne fro the south lyne was descended
> So lowe, that he nas nat, to my sighte,
> Degreës nyne and twenty as in highte.
> Foure of the clokke it was tho, as I gesse:
> For eleven foot, or litel more or lesse,
> My shadwe was at thilke tyme, as there,
> Of swich feet as my lengthe parted were
> In six feet equal of proporcion.
> Ther-with the mones exaltacioun,
> I mene Libra, alwey gan ascende,
> As we were entringe at a thropes ende.

117

The 'thropes' end would seem to mean a suburb, and in this context the phrase can only mean the parish of St Dunstan. It was here that the Pilgrims' Road, or London Road, after failing to hold anything of the Roman straightness as it bobbed up and down through Harbledown, came directly in and turned sharp right for the final approach to the Westgate and the city. Here, too, on the older maps it was joined by the Pilgrims' Way from Winchester, also, at this end, called Pilgrims' Road.

Hasted's account of the Westgate is very much what we can see today, and very much as Chaucer would have known it:

> Westgate was built by Archbishop Sudbury in King Richard II's reign, in the room of an ancient one which was become ruinous over which there was built a church. This gate, situate at the west end of the city, through which the high road passes to London, is the largest and best built of any the city has, making a very handsome appearance, standing between two lofty and spacious round towers, erected in the river on the western side of it. It is built of squared stone, and is embattled and portcullised and machicolated, having a bridge of two arches belonging to the Archbishop, over the western branch of the Stour, adjoining it.

We have nothing in any of the surviving manuscripts which describes a stay in Canterbury and the return journey, although some ingenious attempts have been made to supply this want of evidence. Chaucer clearly had intended the double journey from the number of stories that were anticipated from the thirty pilgrims (if we include the Canon's Yeoman). He seems to have done a certain amount of rearrangement in the hope of overcoming what is an apparently insuperable problem of anticlimax after the 'Holy Blisful Martir' had been found.

For the pilgrims, the arrival at Canterbury would have been, in a sense, a new beginning. The travellers would have visited a circuit of shrines and holy places, and while they were there

Canterbury Grey Friars. The city became a favourite place for the mendicant orders soon after they first came to England. Arriving after the monks had long built up their houses in important towns, these Franciscan and other friars had to compete for scarce building sites. The house seen here stretches out over the river Stour. *Photo: Jill Waterhouse*

Overleaf: Christ Church Great Gate, giving access to the Cathedral precincts at Canterbury. This detail above the pedestrian entrance shows the wonderful carving in the pre-Reformation stonework. *Photo: Jill Waterhouse.*

119

Above: Canterbury Cathedral: An interior view of the nave. This was being rebuilt in Chaucer's time, and was designed by Henry Yevele, royal master-mason to both Edward III and Richard II. It is a wonderful example of Perpendicular architecture, the soaring arches a contrast to the sturdier arches of Rochester Cathedral's Norman nave. *Photo: John Crampton*

122

they might well have paid attention to other pilgrim centres in Canterbury as well as the shrine itself, and the other altars associated with Becket in the Cathedral. All seem to have been intending to return to London as far as we know, but we have no particular reason for thinking that they would necessarily go back as one party, except for the promised dinner in honour of the best Tale.

In the Cathedral and City as we see them today there have been many changes since Chaucer's time, but the essential plan of the medieval walled City would be recognisable to him, and the Westgate and part of the circuit wall still stand. Many of the religious foundations of his time have left no visible traces, but there are substantial ruins of the Benedictine St Augustine's Abbey, of Grey Friars and Black Friars. From the air, despite ring roads and much twentieth century expansion and re-development, the main features of the old City can easily be discerned.

Within the Cathedral precincts, Christ Church Gate, giving access, dates from the eve of the Reformation. The cloisters of the Cathedral Monastery, along which Becket walked for the last time, were rebuilt after his death but would be recognisable to Chaucer. The Cathedral itself he would find rather different: the central tower is late medieval and the north-west tower

Overleaf: St Augustine's Abbey, Canterbury. Founded on a former pagan site in 598, the year after the mission of Augustine to England, it was dedicated to St Peter and St Paul. Like the Cathedral monastery, it was a Benedictine (Black Monk) house. Augustine and his first bishops, as well as the early kings and queens of Kent, were given their first burial here. The original small complex of Saxon buildings was completely replaced after the Norman Conquest by the structure whose remains we see today, and the monks' quarters were further modified after the Dissolution when they were incorporated in a King's House. The Abbey buildings were demolished. The remains of the nave can be seen on the right of the photograph, and in the distance, the Bell Harry Tower of Canterbury Cathedral surveys its fallen rival. *Photo: S. & O. Mathews*

123

nineteenth century, and the nave was being rebuilt during his lifetime. The great shrine, chief goal of the pilgrims, was of course dismantled in 1538 by Henry VIII, and the other sacred places are much altered.

A supplementary Tale, not by Chaucer, suggests that the pilgrims might have stayed at the Chequers of Hope Inn in the High Street. If nothing else, this tells us that it was a known lodging house for pilgrims at the time.

Opposite: The Chapel of St Anselm, on the south side of Canterbury Cathedral, still shows much Norman work. *Photo: Jill Waterhouse*

My Tale is Doon

Our attempt to follow the journey as Chaucer seems to have imagined it produced much more than we twentieth-century travellers thought possible before setting out. The early parts of the route through London have been frozen by the years far into the suburbs in bricks and mortar. Between Dartford Brent and Rochester there are difficulties where Watling Street has been altered several times. Thereafter, the difficulties are not from lack of information, but from a surfeit: as well as the Roman road, we are offered too many alternative possibilities in the form of parallel ways, like that through the woods at Cobham, or the route occupied in the nineteenth century by the railway line north of Faversham and Sittingbourne, for any kind of certainty as to pilgrims' ways. And yet in the area of most confusion, Harbledown on the western approaches to Canterbury, we get the weightiest testimony of all as to the 'cult' route being used by pilgrims while pilgrimages were still permitted—from the great Erasmus himself.

Each age of route-making has left its own signature on the map, and in its time each has had its own 'Network South-East'. Canterbury seems to have been the centre of such a network first in prehistoric, then Roman, and later medieval times; later

128

still in the days of coach and horses, the railway age, and the tyranny of the internal combustion engine.

All these societies contributed to the landscape of today, and it is through this landscape that we probably get to know as much as we ever shall know of many of them. Their contributions were negative as well as positive, but they seem to have left the landscape less scarred than we have.

COBHAM TO ROCHESTER

An old track that takes an almost exactly parallel course south of Watling
Street as it nears Rochester. The track passes through the village of
Cobham as its main street, and then carries on as a lane across fields and
through the woods of Cobham Park, curving up towards Watling Street to
join it for the approach to the bridge over the Medway. It is cut off by the
M2 and the overspill from Rochester before it can reach the Roman road.
From either side of Cobham two clear tracks run north to join Watling
Street, one a bridleway, the other Cobham's main access to the highway.
These short tracks linking a greenway with the Roman road are a typical
feature. © *Crown copyright*

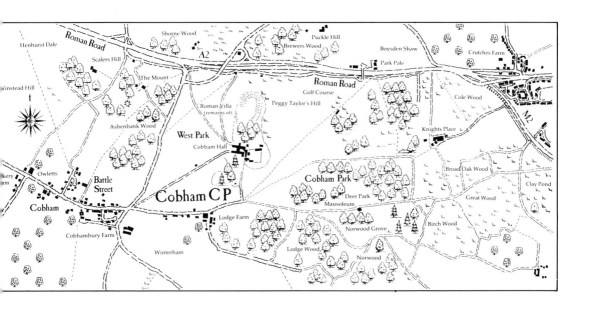

ROADS AT NEWINGTON

The greenway from Gillingham runs north of Watling Street and absolutely parallel from Breach to Newington. It passes through the village as its main street, while the Roman road cuts through the more modern development. East of Newington the track is lost briefly, but it reappears in the form of the railway which, curving up from Newington station, makes use of it for most of its journey towards Sittingbourne. As at Cobham, the short tracks connecting greenway and Roman road are easily seen, although they have been adapted to different uses over the centuries. © *Crown copyright*

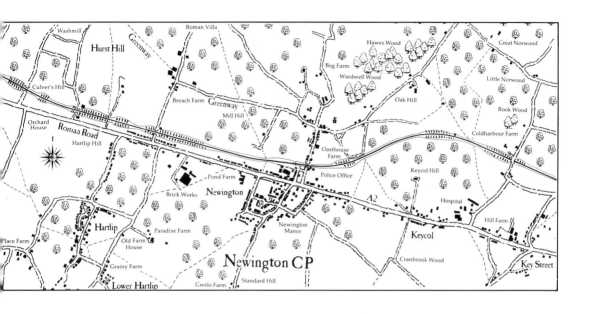

PILGRIMS' ROUTES TO FAVERSHAM

Here we can see a clear example of a parallel road which has been appropriated by the railway. From the left Watling Street runs diagonally straight across the map towards Ospringe. Above it, the railway line, with a very minor road close beside it, follows the escarpment, swinging away from the parallel road to come close to Watling Street at Faversham Station. The track, meanwhile, takes a straighter route through Bysing Wood to enter Faversham farther north. Near centre top can be seen the ruined church in a field above the railway line, close to Deerton Street, while the ancient Stone Church, west of Ospringe, is south of the railway line near the bottom right-hand corner. © *Crown copyright*

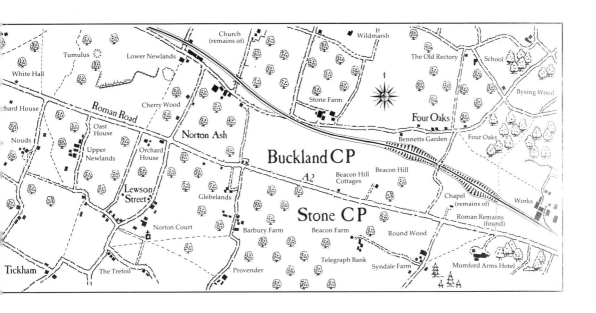

HARBLEDOWN TO CANTERBURY

A complicated maze of roads, lanes and tracks leading through Harbledown and on to Canterbury. At Upper Harbledown the A2 swings away from Watling Street and bypasses Harbledown and Canterbury, while the Roman road, a minor road for a short stretch, changes alignment twice as it negotiates the hilly country before running down to Canterbury. An offshoot from the A2 confuses matters by crossing and recrossing Watling Street. High up in Church Wood, above Harbledown, an old trackway takes a course parallel to the Roman road leading towards Canterbury, and further west a number of short tracks lead down from it to meet the Roman road. From the south-west, the North Downs Way can be seen passing under the A2 and coming north to meet Watling Street at Harbledown. © *Crown copyright*

136

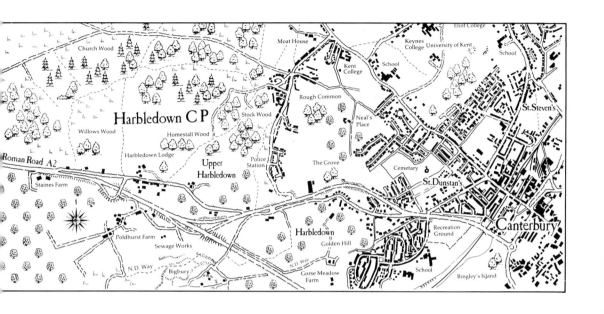

Sources of Local
Information

Southwark Local Studies Library, 211 Borough High Street,
London SE11 1JA. Tel: 01-403 3507
The library holds a collection of material illustrating the history
of the borough.

Greenwich Local History Library, Woodlands, 90 Mycenae
Road, Blackheath, London SE3.

Dartford Local Studies Library, Central Library, Central Park,
Dartford, Kent, DA1 1EU. Tel: (0322) 21133
The library holds archive material on the history of the town
and publishes a series of Local History Leaflets.

The Gravesham Local Collection, Central Library, Windmill
Street, Gravesend, Kent, DA12 1AQ. Tel: (0474) 52758/65600.
The collection contains an extensive range of material on the
Gravesend/Northfleet area, including Cobham.

Rochester Library, Northgate, Rochester, Kent. Tel: (0634)
42415
The library holds a wide selection of material on Roman and
medieval Rochester.

The Faversham Society, Fleur de Lis Heritage Centre, 12
  Preston Street, Faversham, Kent ME13 8NS. Tel: (0795)
  534542
The centre covers 1,000 years of history in the area of
Faversham and Ospringe, with award-winning displays, a
well-stocked bookshop and a series of local history mono-
graphs published by the Society.

Canterbury Central Library, High Street, Canterbury, Kent,
  CT1 2JF. Tel: (0227) 463608/69964
There is a large collection on the history of Canterbury. The city
is well-stocked with museums, and the Pilgrims' Way Centre
in St. Margaret's Street offers a 'living history' exhibition that
takes the visitor on a realistic pilgrimage from London to
Canterbury.

Suggestions For Further Reading

Chaucer

The Canterbury Tales, edited by W. W. Skeat. World Classics, Oxford University Press.

Chaucer and his England, by G. G. Coulton. London, 3rd ed., 1921.

Chaucer and the Fifteenth Century, by H. S. Bennett. Oxford University Press, 1947.

Chaucer and his World, by Derek Brewer, Eyre Methuen, 1978.

Chaucer's World, by Edith Rickert, edited by C. C. Olsen and M. M. Crow. New York and London, 1948.

Background and History

ROMAN

Britannia, by S. S. Frere. Routledge & Kegan Paul, 1978.

The Coming of Rome, by John Wacher. Routledge & Kegan Paul, 1978.

Later Roman Britain, by Stephen Johnson. Routledge & Kegan Paul.

Roman Roads in Britain, by I. D. Margary. Volumes I and II, 1955 and 1957.

140

MEDIEVAL

Anglo-Saxon England, by Lloyd and Jennifer Laing. Routledge & Kegan Paul.

The Fourteenth Century, by M. McKisack. Oxford University Press, 1959.

Thomas Becket, by Richard Winston. Constable, 1967.

Medieval People, by Eileen Power. London, 1924.

Medieval Monasteries of Great Britain, by Lionel Butler and Chris Given-Wilson. Michael Joseph, 1979.

Concise Oxford Dictionary of English Place-Names, by E. Ekwall. Oxford University Press, 4th ed., 1960.

LANDSCAPE

The Making of the English Landscape, by W. G. Hoskins. Pelican Books, 2nd ed., 1976.

Landscape Archaeology, by M. Aston and T. Rowley. David & Charles, 1974.

History on the Ground, by M. W. Beresford. Methuen, rev. ed., 1976.

Fields in the English Landscape, by Christopher Taylor, J. M. Dent, 1975.

Villages in the Landscape, by Trevor Rowley. J. M. Dent, 1978.

Medieval England: An Aerial Survey, by M. W. Beresford and J. K. S. St. Joseph, Cambridge University Press, 2nd ed., 1979.

The Road to Canterbury

The Canterbury Pilgrimages, by H. S. Ward. London, 1904.

In Kentish Pilgrim Land: Its ancient roads and shrines, by William Coles Finch. 1925.

The Buildings of England: West Kent and the Weald, ed. Nicolaus Pevsner. *North East and East Kent*, ed. Nicolaus Pevsner and John Newman. Penguin Books.

Camden's Britannia: Kent, edited by Gordon J. Copley. Hutchinson, 1977.

History of Kent, by F. W. Jessup, London, 1958.

Kentish Place Names, by J. K. Wallenberg. 1931.

Some Notes on the Road from London to Canterbury in the Middle Ages, by Henry Littlehales, 1898.

Dartford Parish Church, by G. H. Porteus. Dartford Local History Leaflets No. 4.

Medieval Dartford, 1200–1500, by Peter W. Boreham. Dartford Local History Leaflets No. 15.

The Lords of Cobham Hall, by Esme Wingfield Stratford. Cassell & Co., 1954.

Cobham, by Tom Dymond. Published for Cobham Parish Council by Meresborough Books.

Excavations at Faversham, 1965, by B. Philp. 1968.

Faversham Abbey and Its Last Abbot, John Caslock, by the late Canon W. Telfer. Faversham Papers, 1965.

Boughton-under-Blean, by Joan White. Faversham Papers, 1983.

Canterbury Cathedral, by D. I. Hill. Bell & Hyman, 1986.

St. Augustine's Abbey, Canterbury, by A. Clapham. Official Guide, 1955.

LOCAL HISTORY JOURNALS
Archaeologia Cantiana
Journal of Kent Local History
Bygone Kent
Kent Companion

Index

(numbers in italics indicate illustrations)

143